Wedding Romance

A hand-drawn coloring book

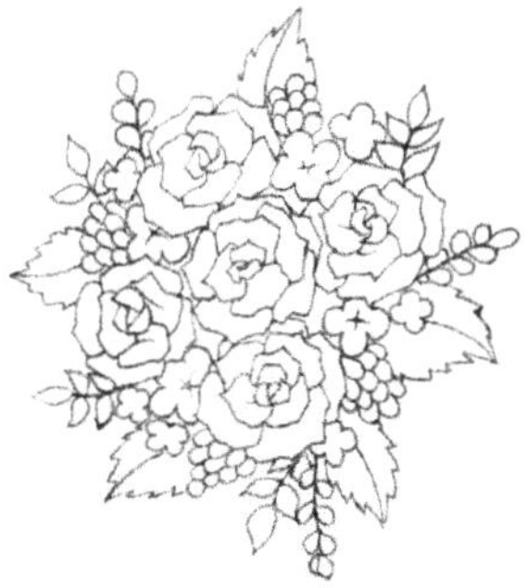

Queenie Wong

ISBN-13: 978-1534892682
ISBN-10: 1534892680
First published in United States in 2016
Illustrations by Queenie Wong
Wonger0050@yahoo.com.hk

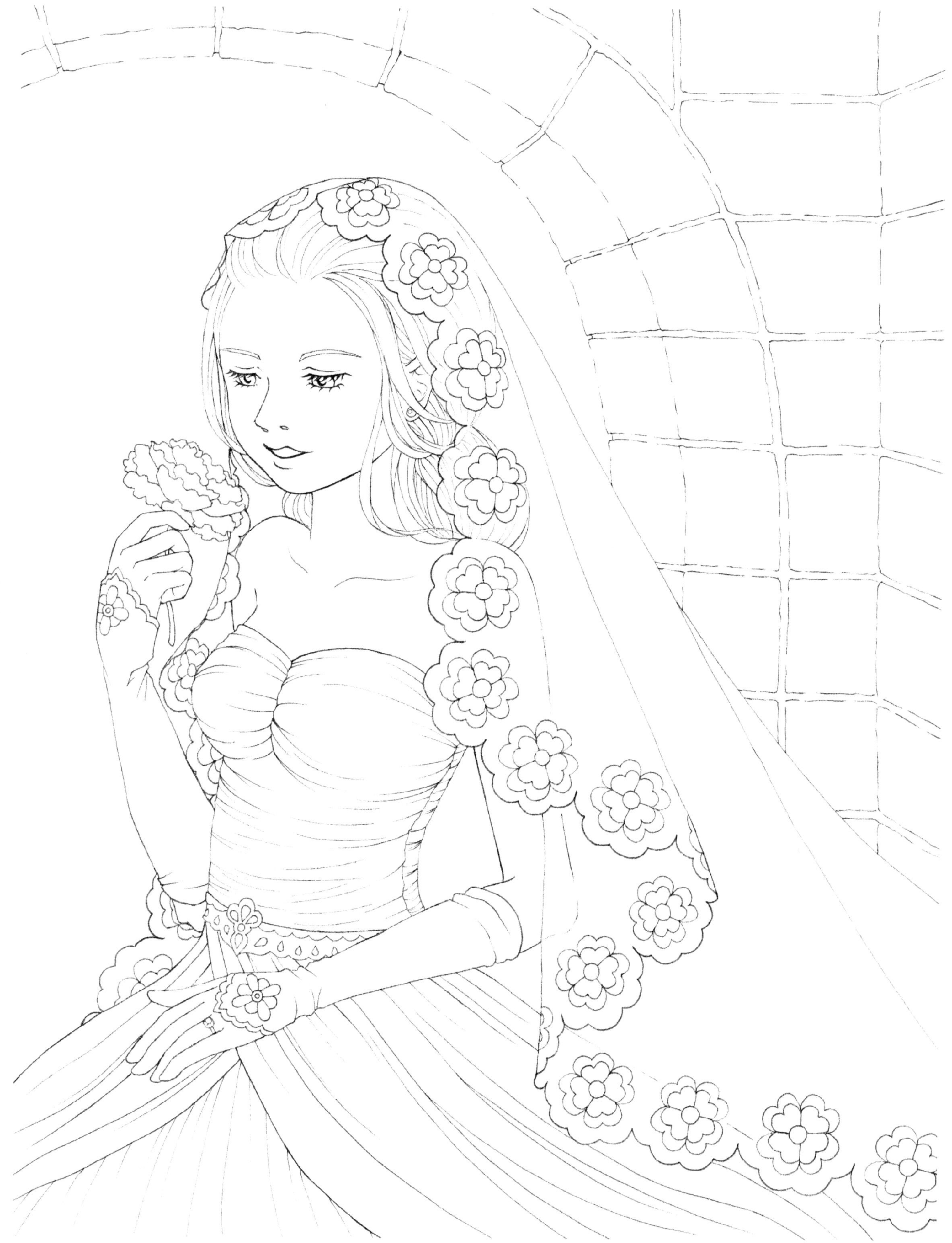

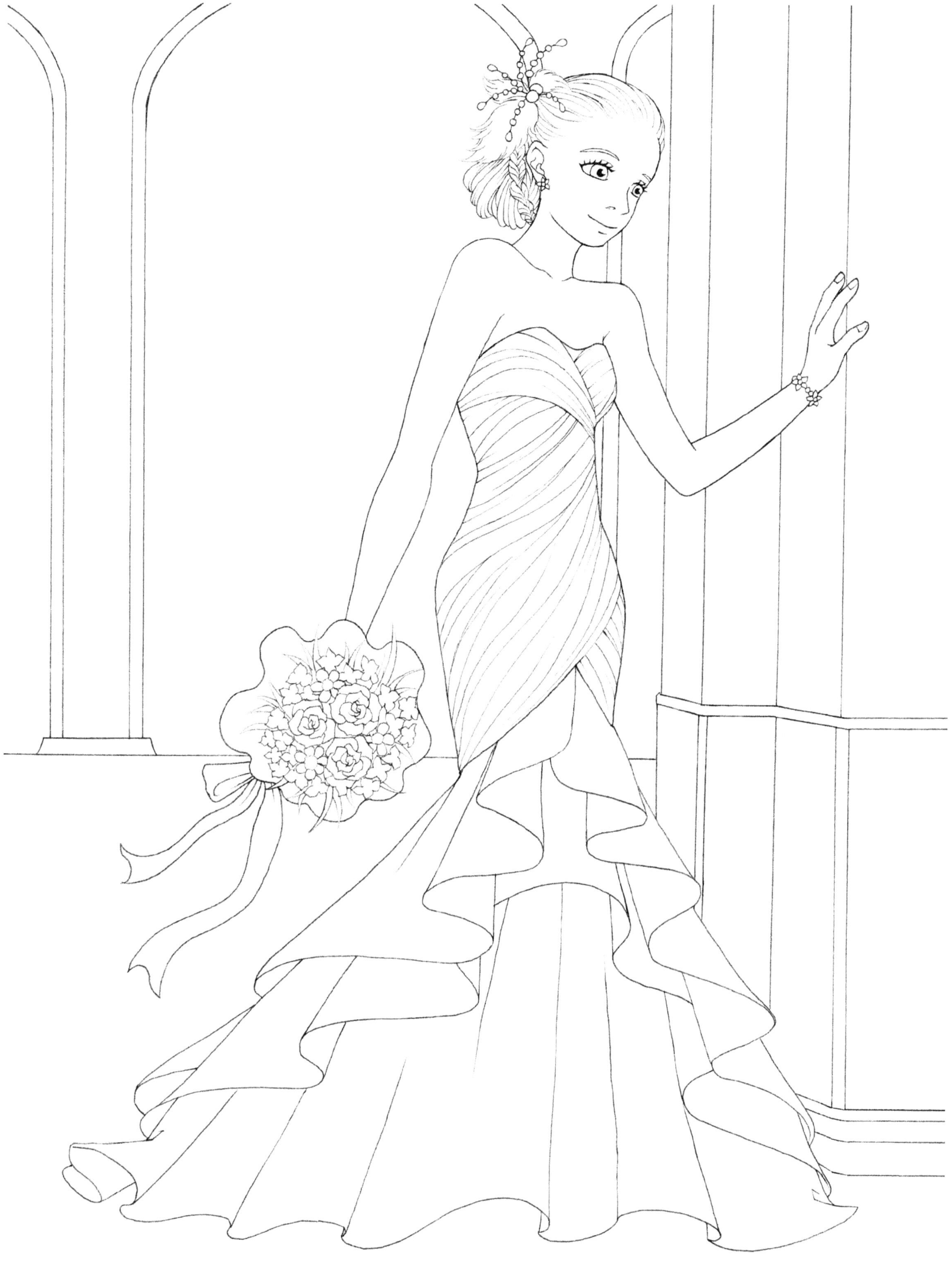

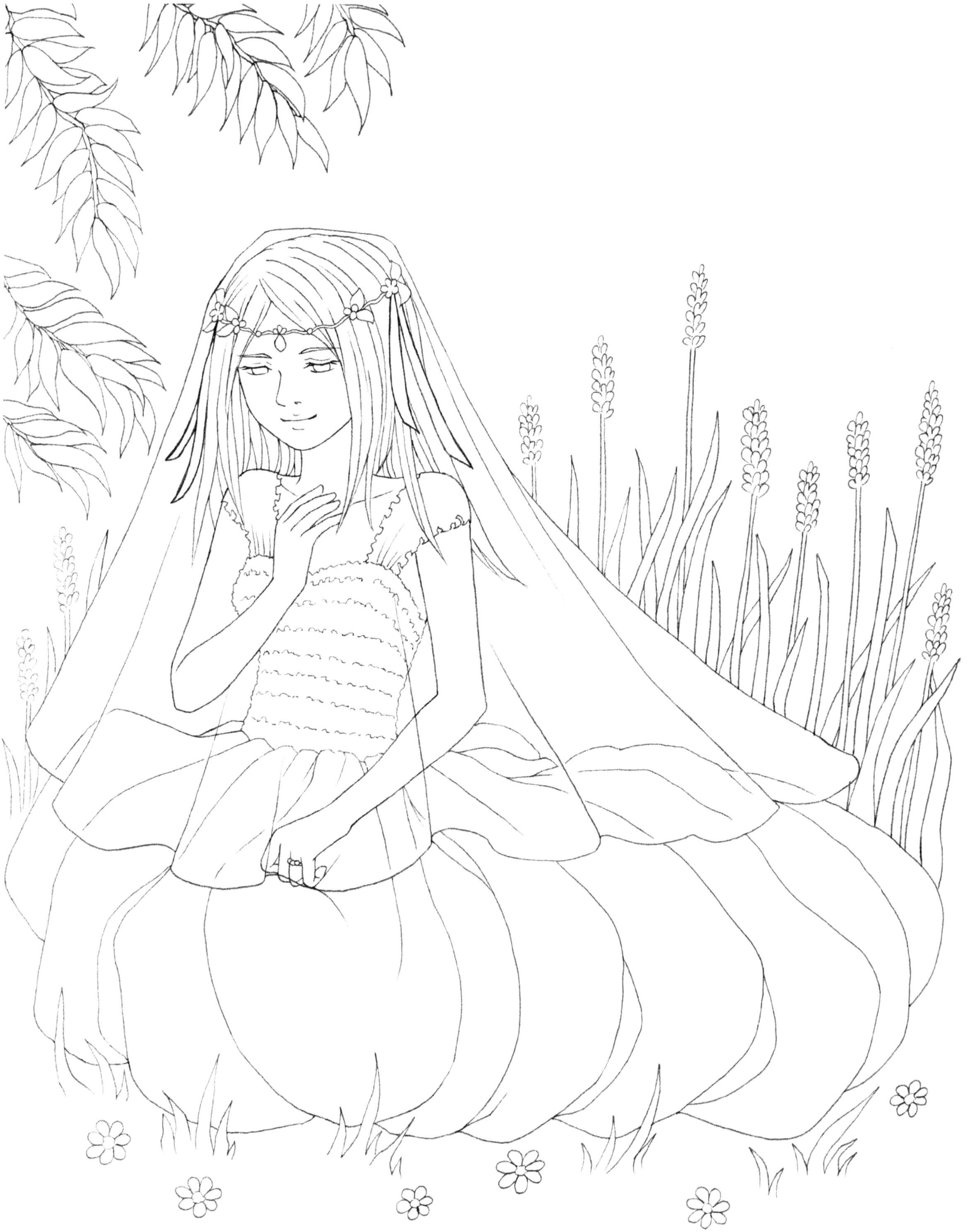

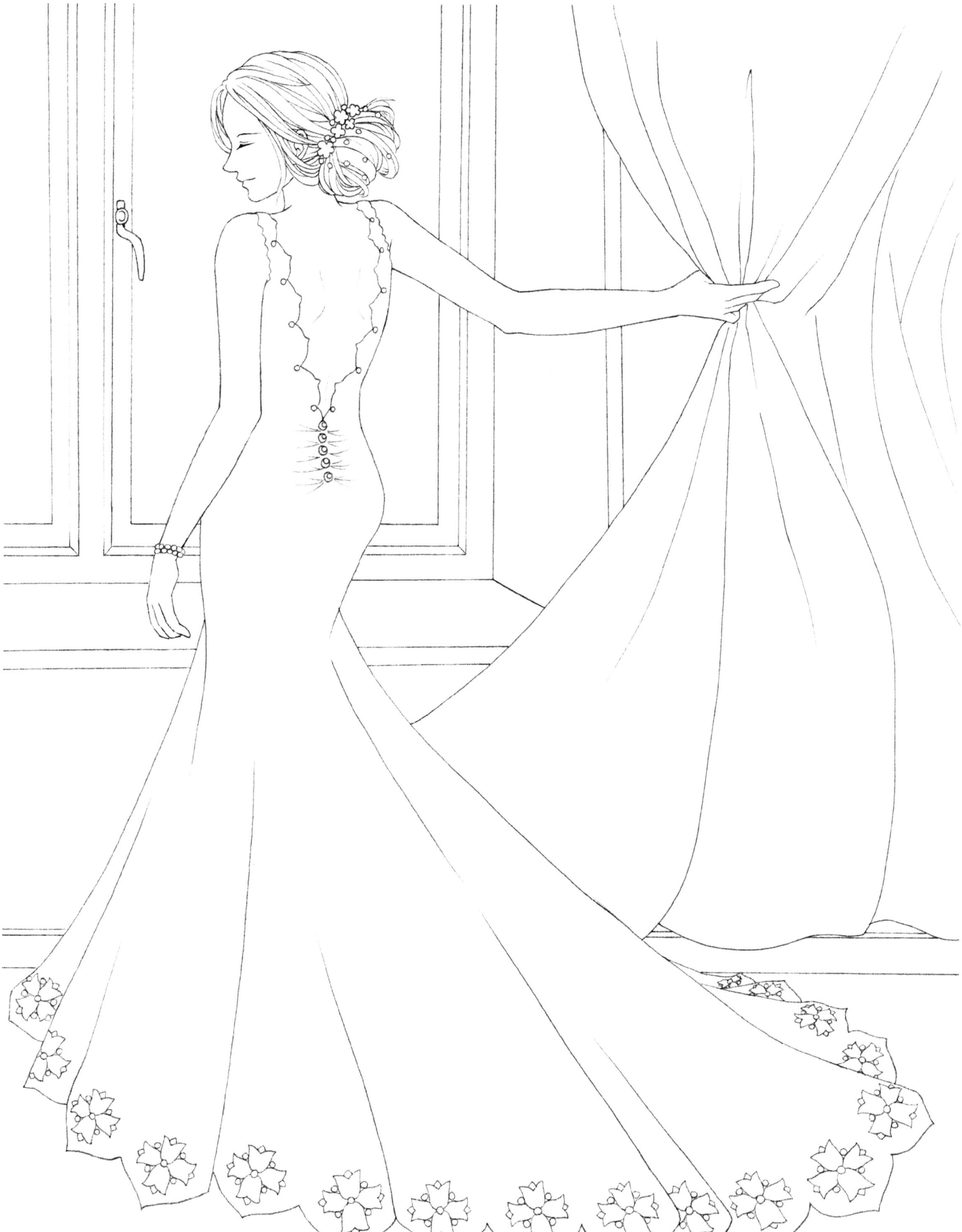

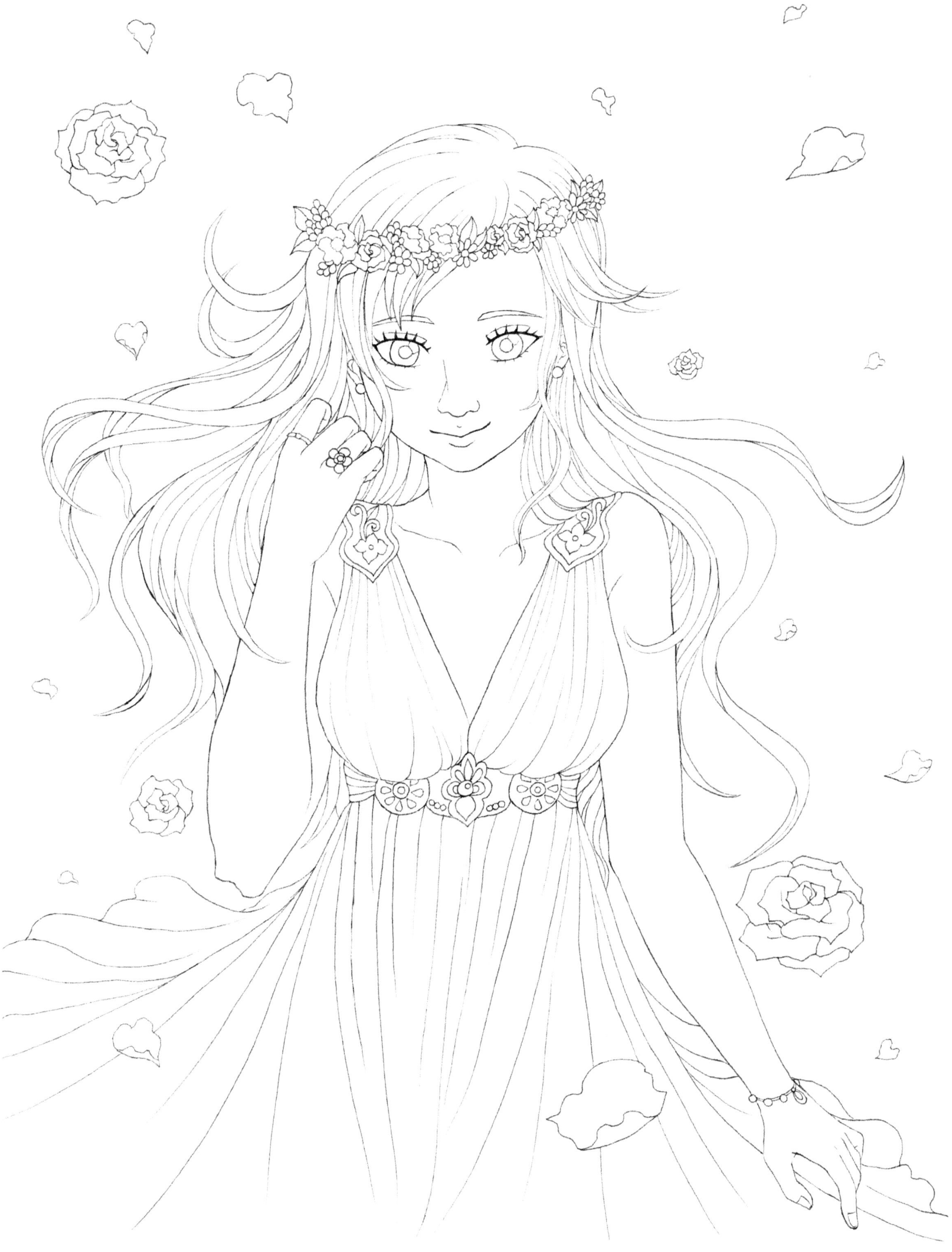

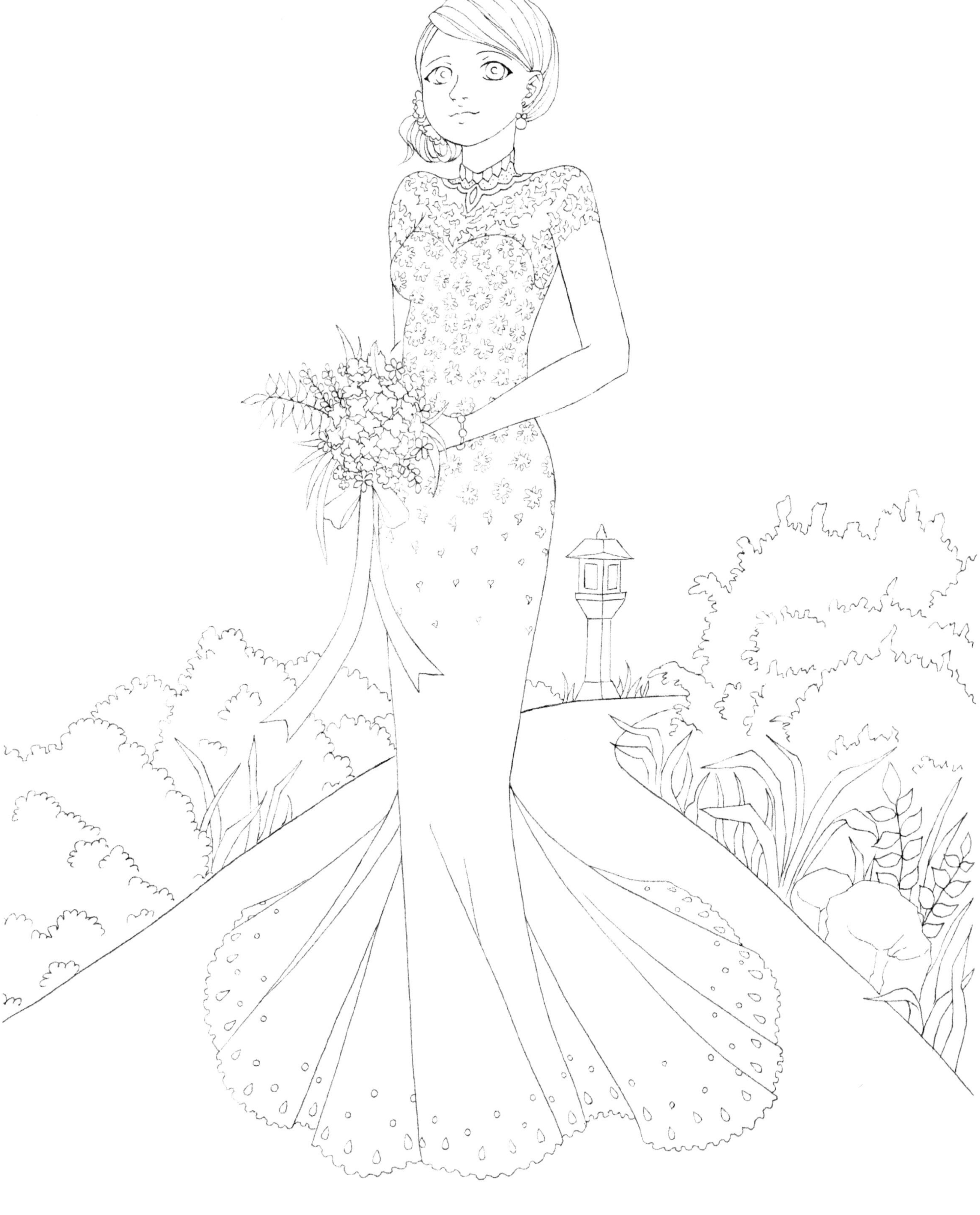

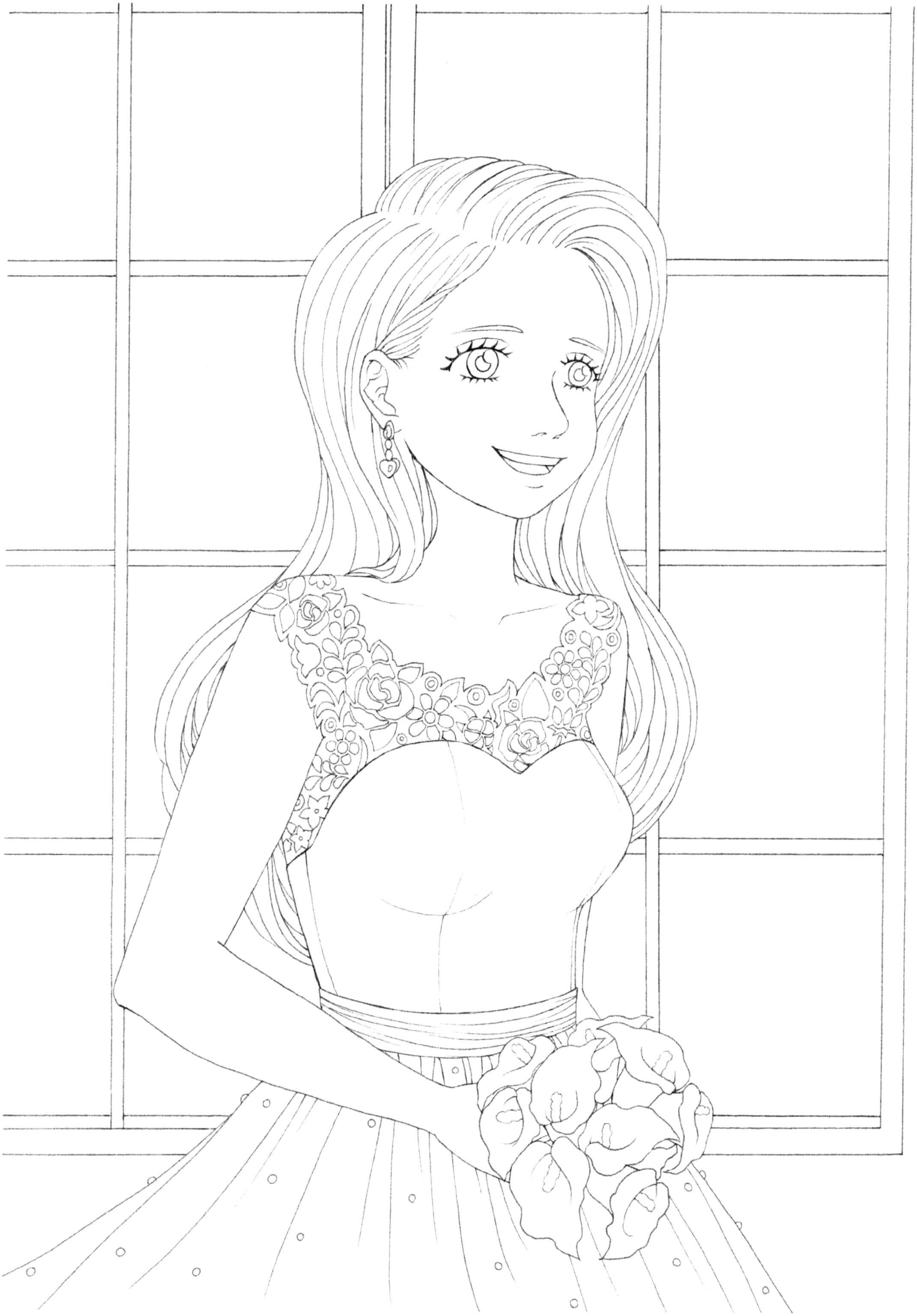

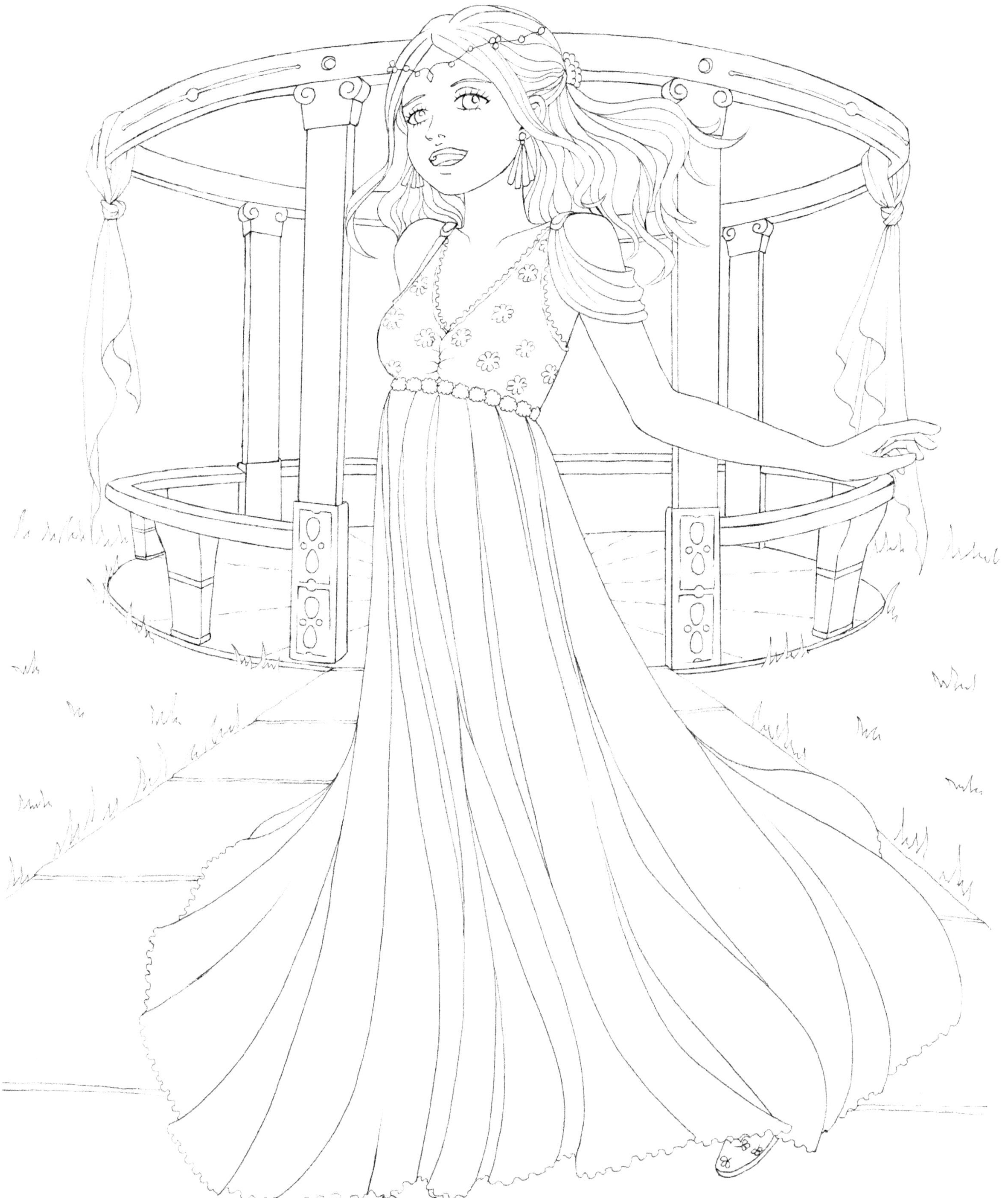

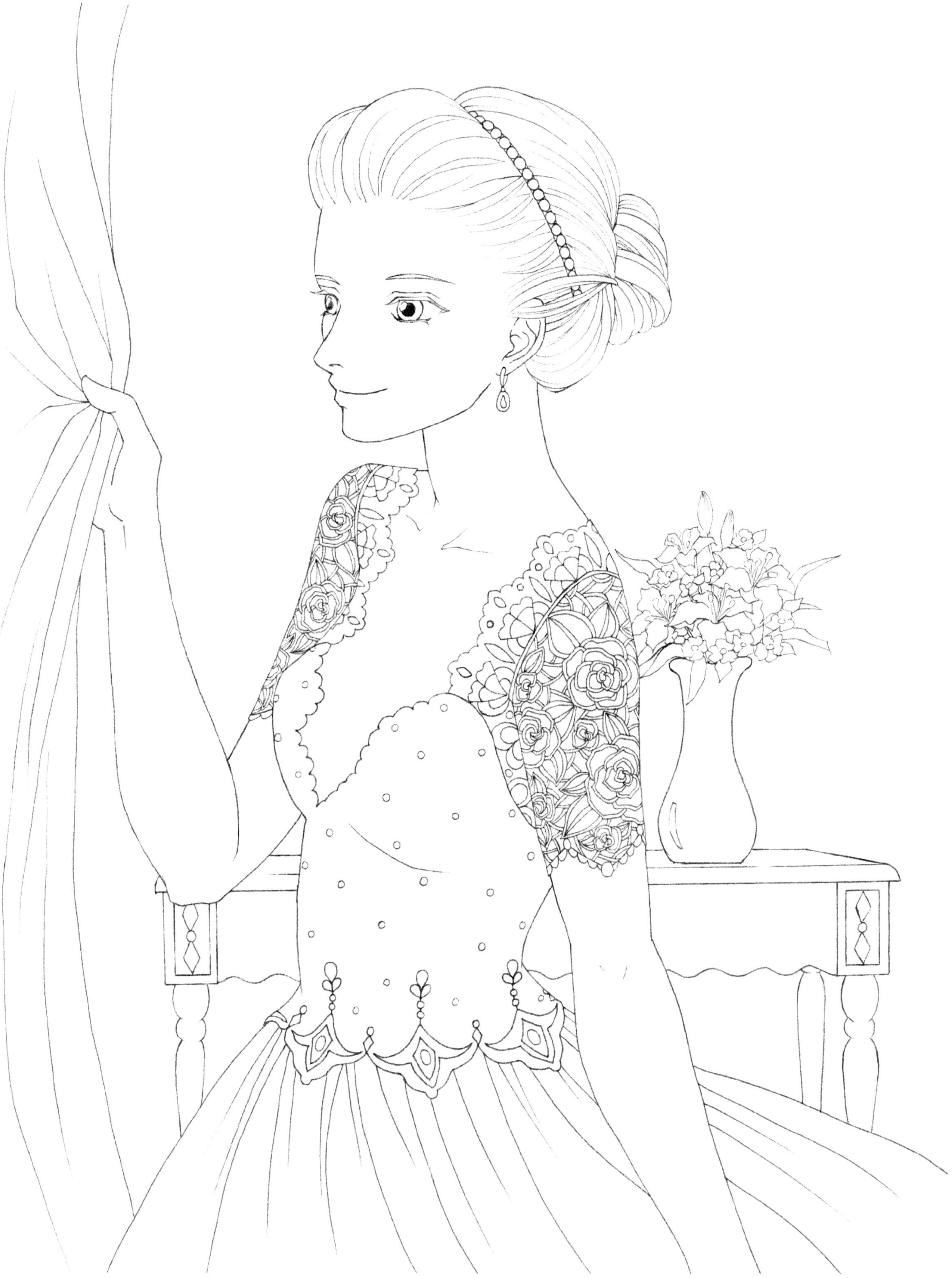

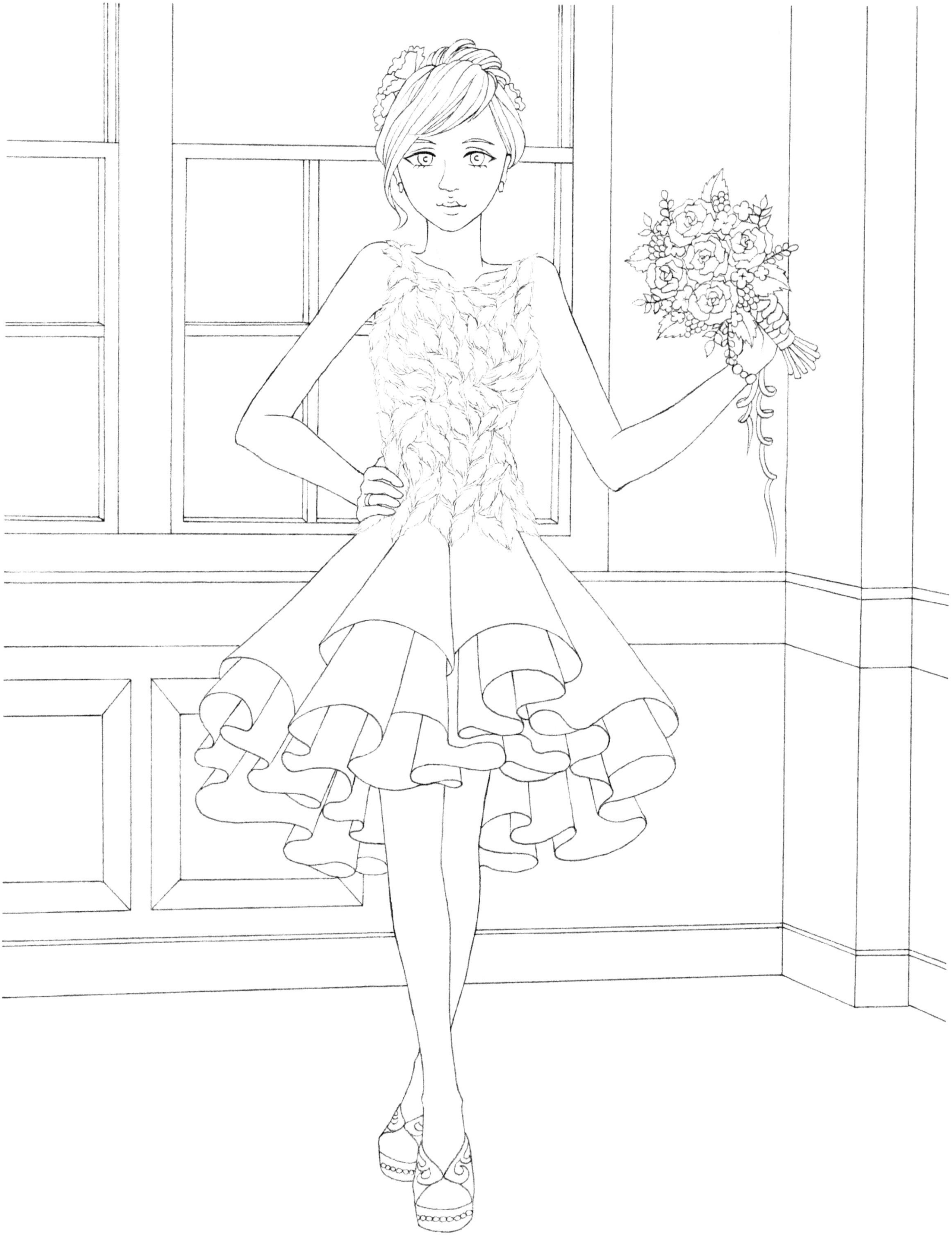

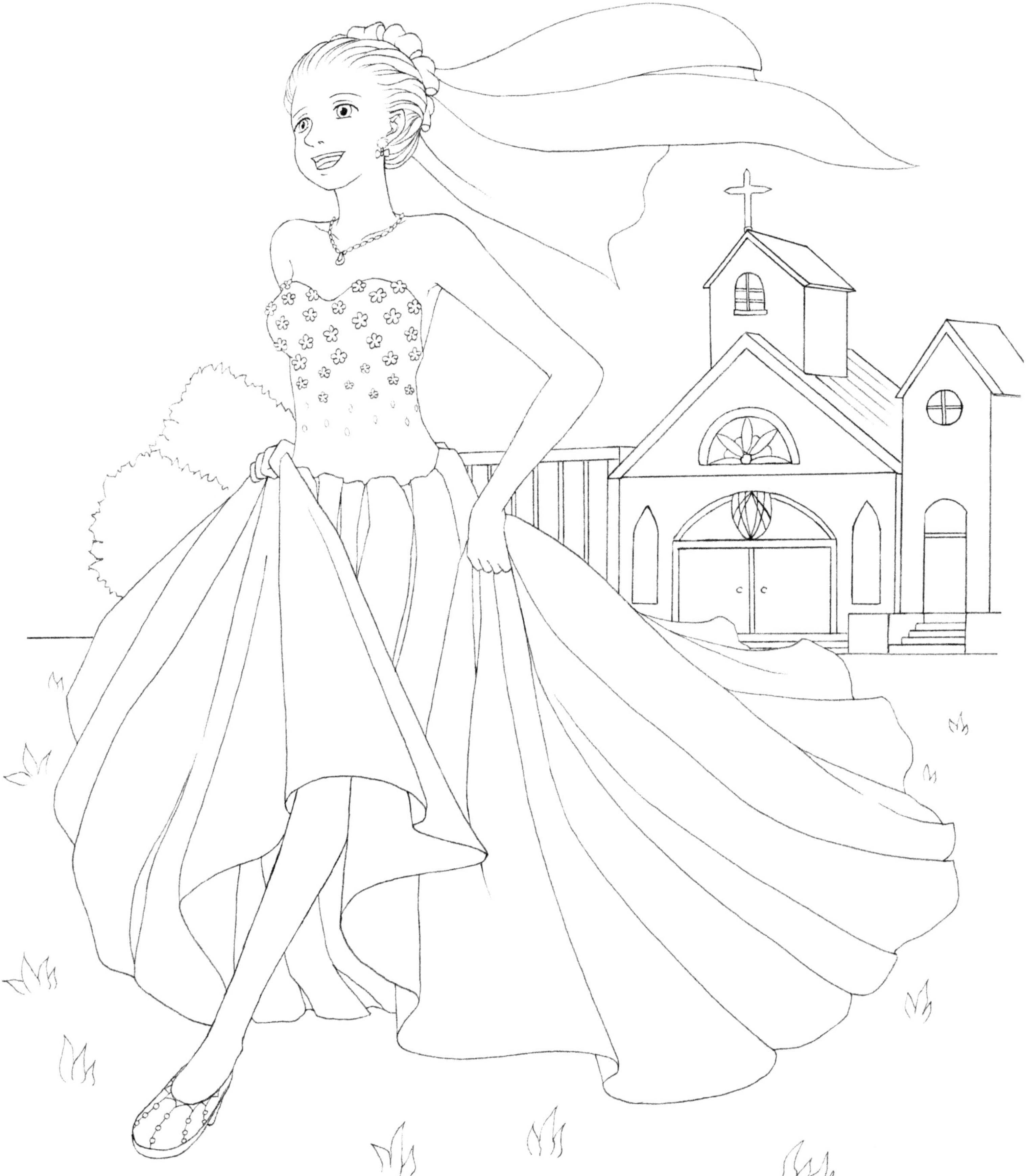

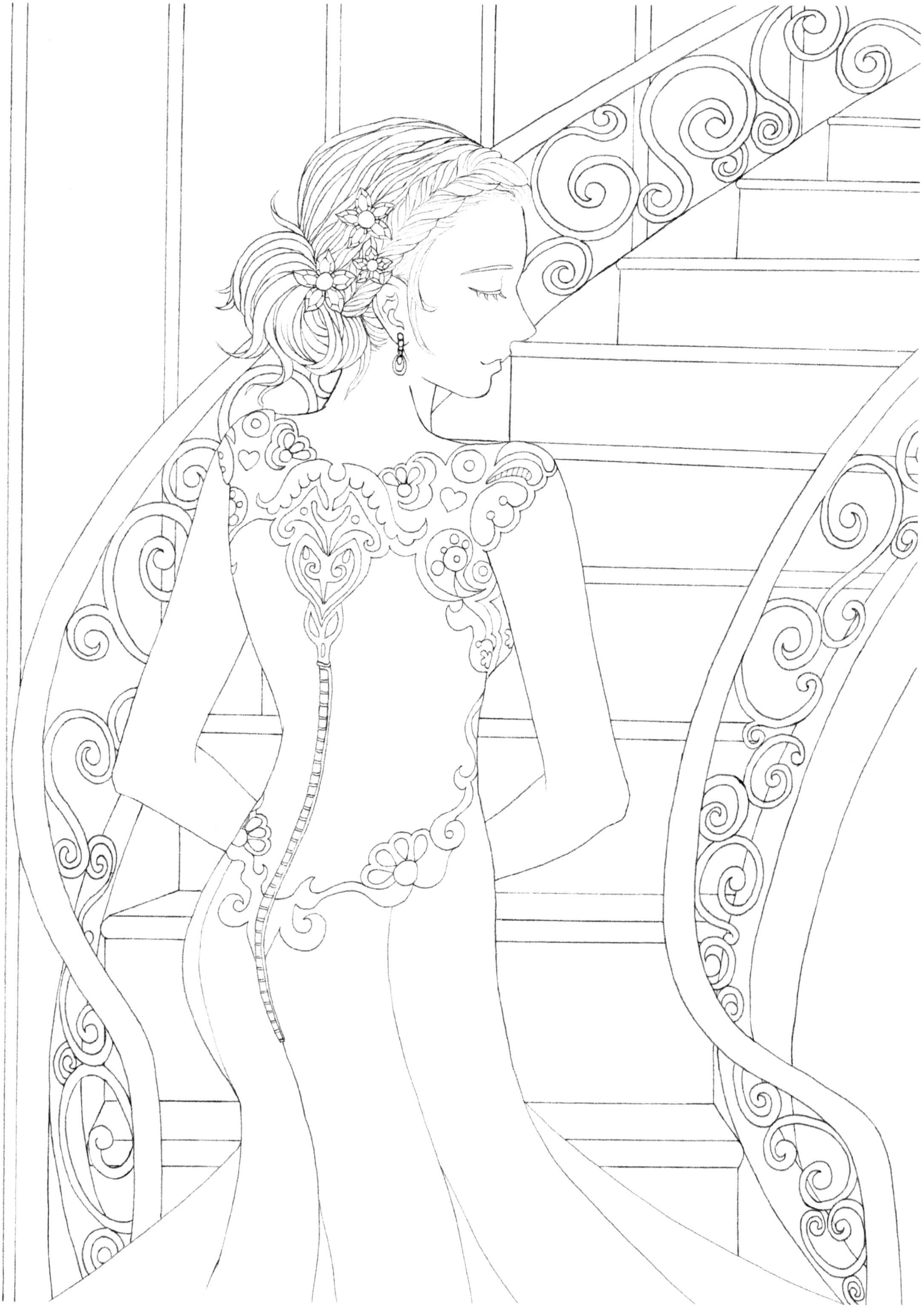

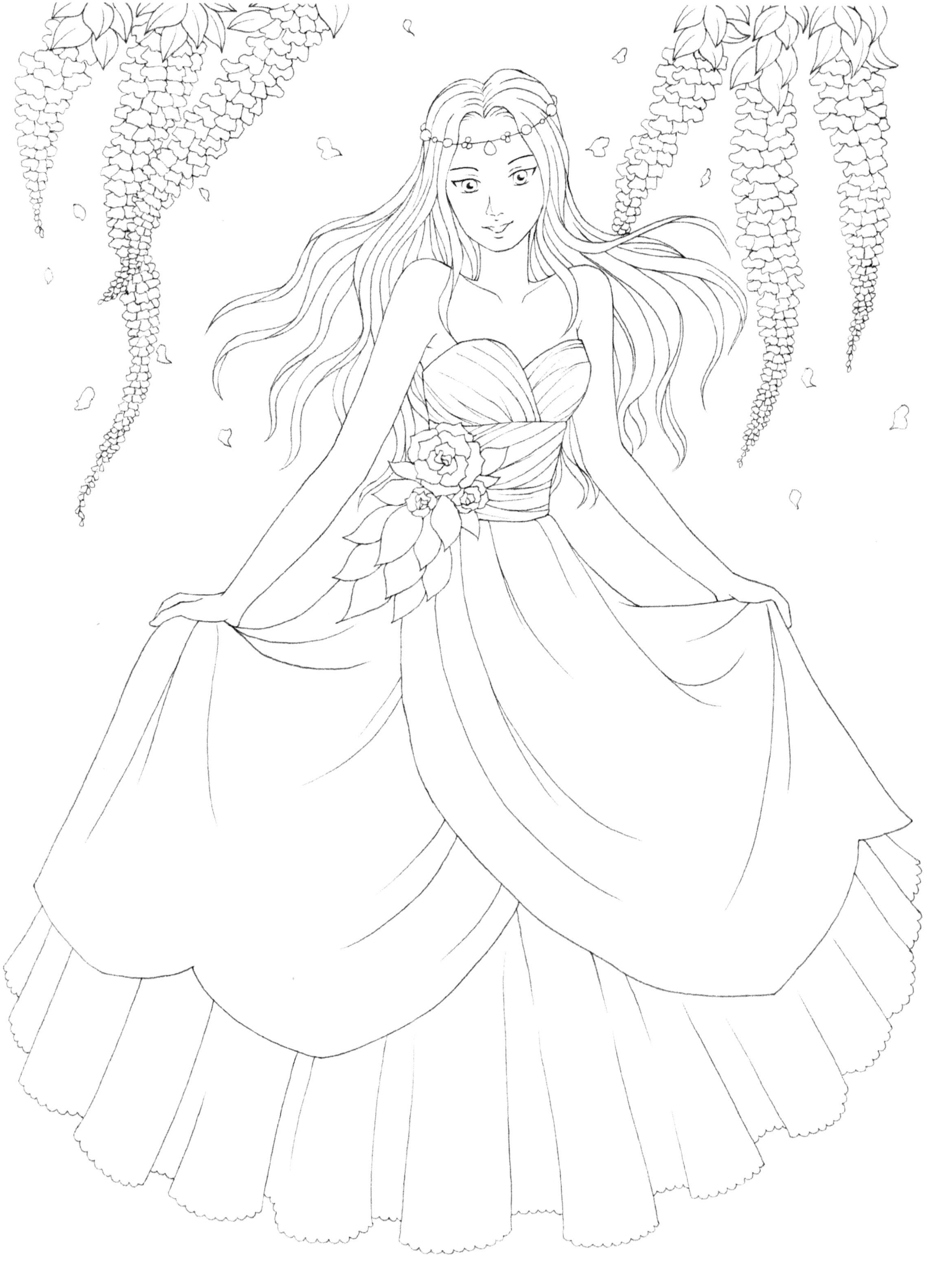

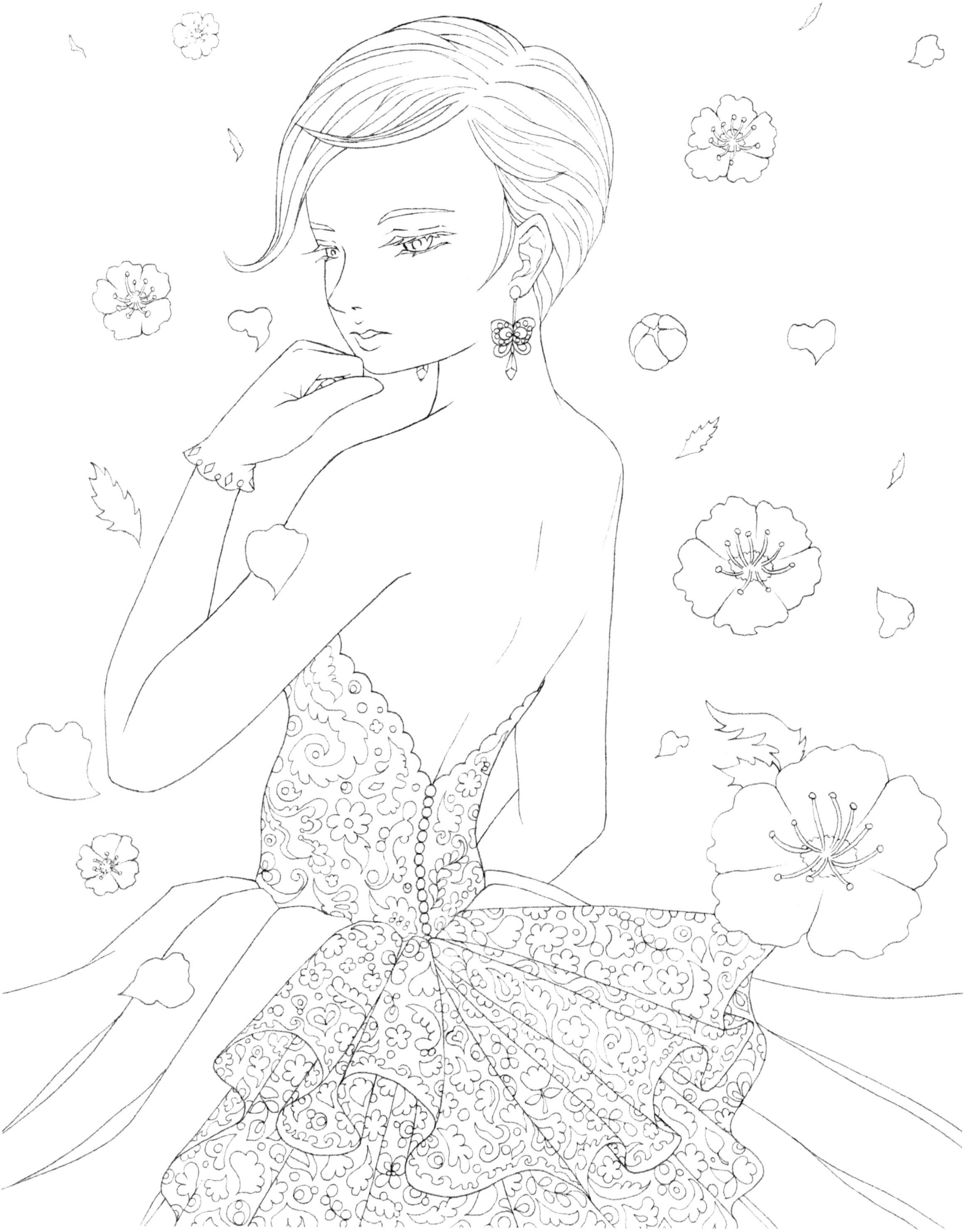

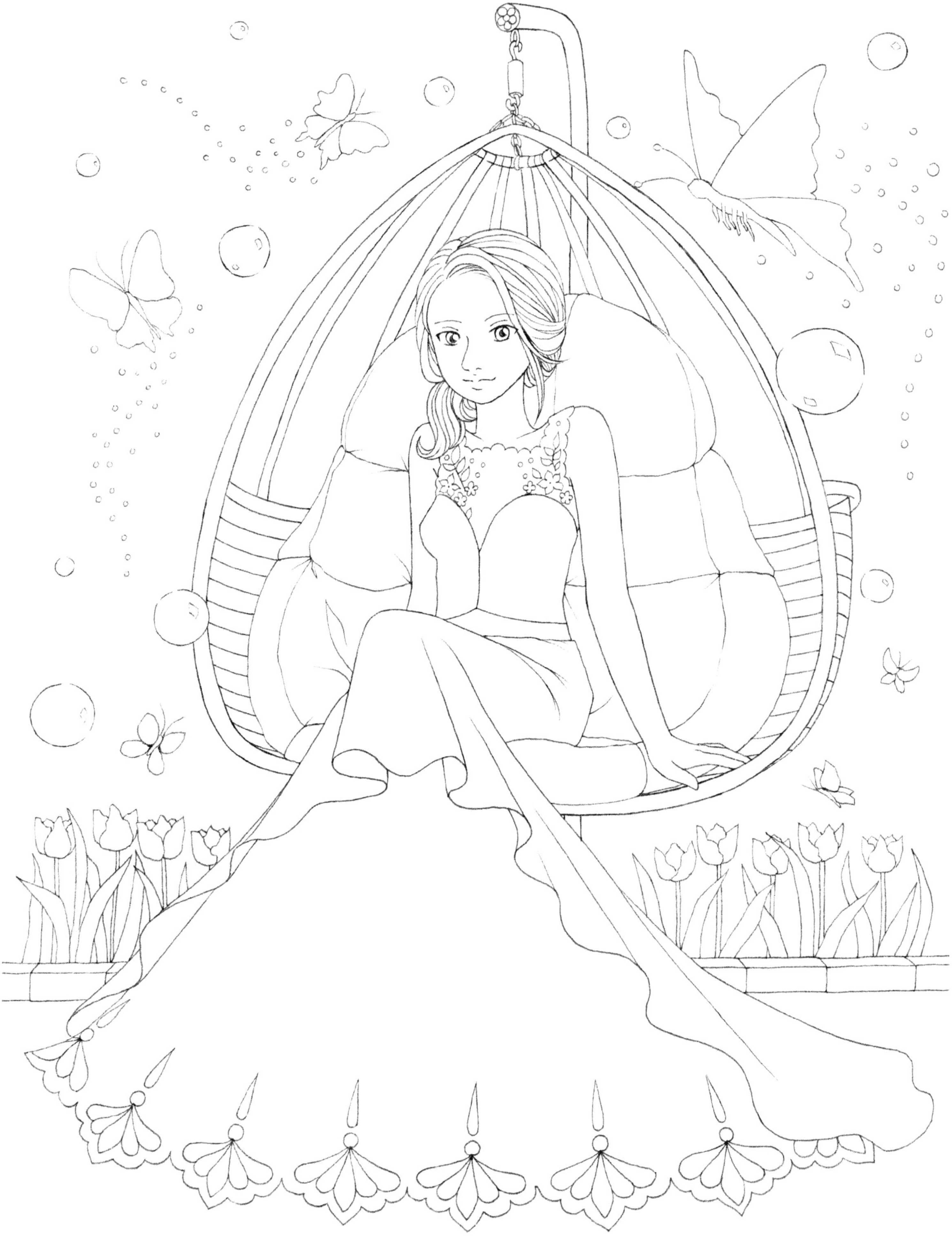

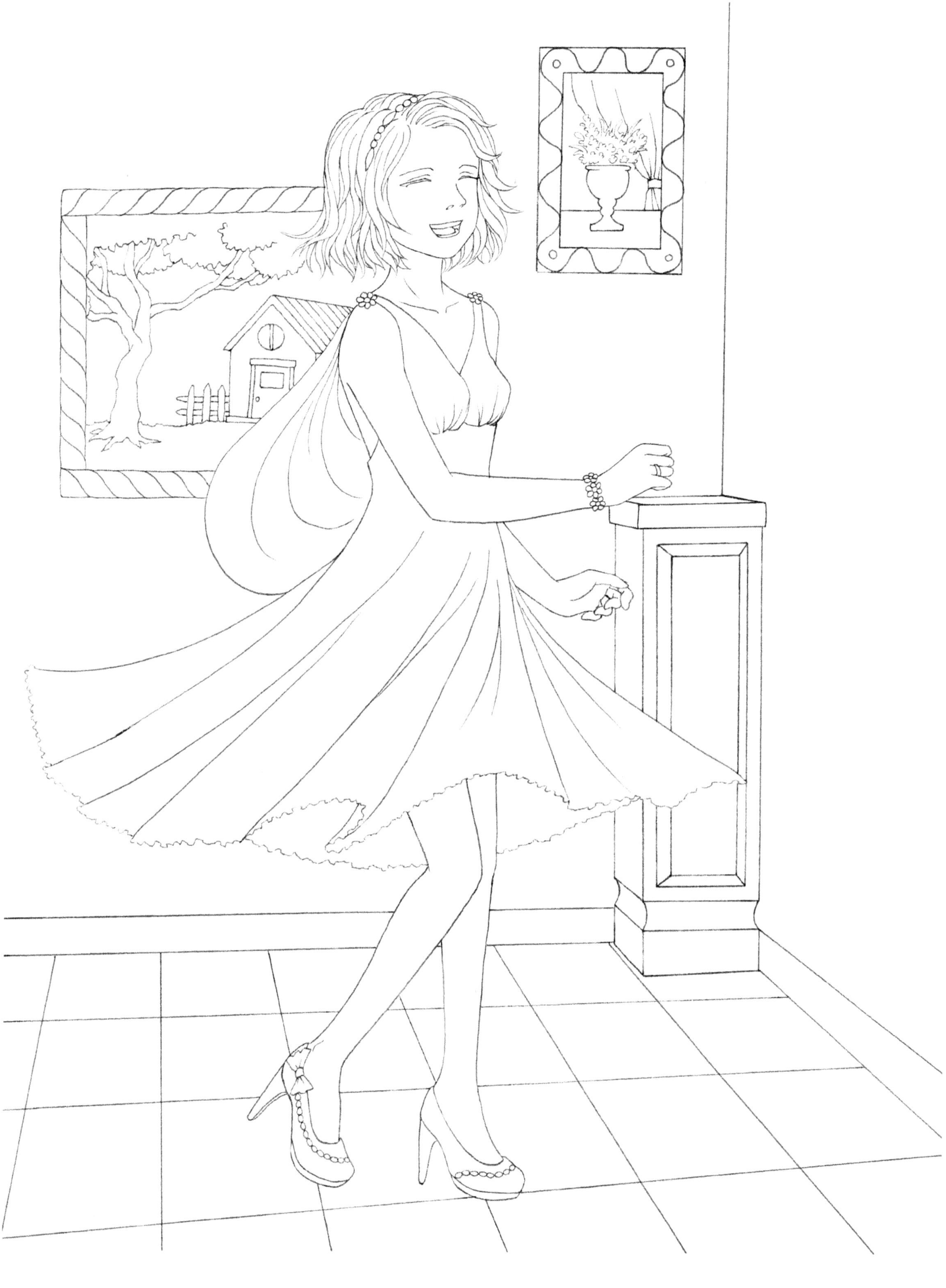

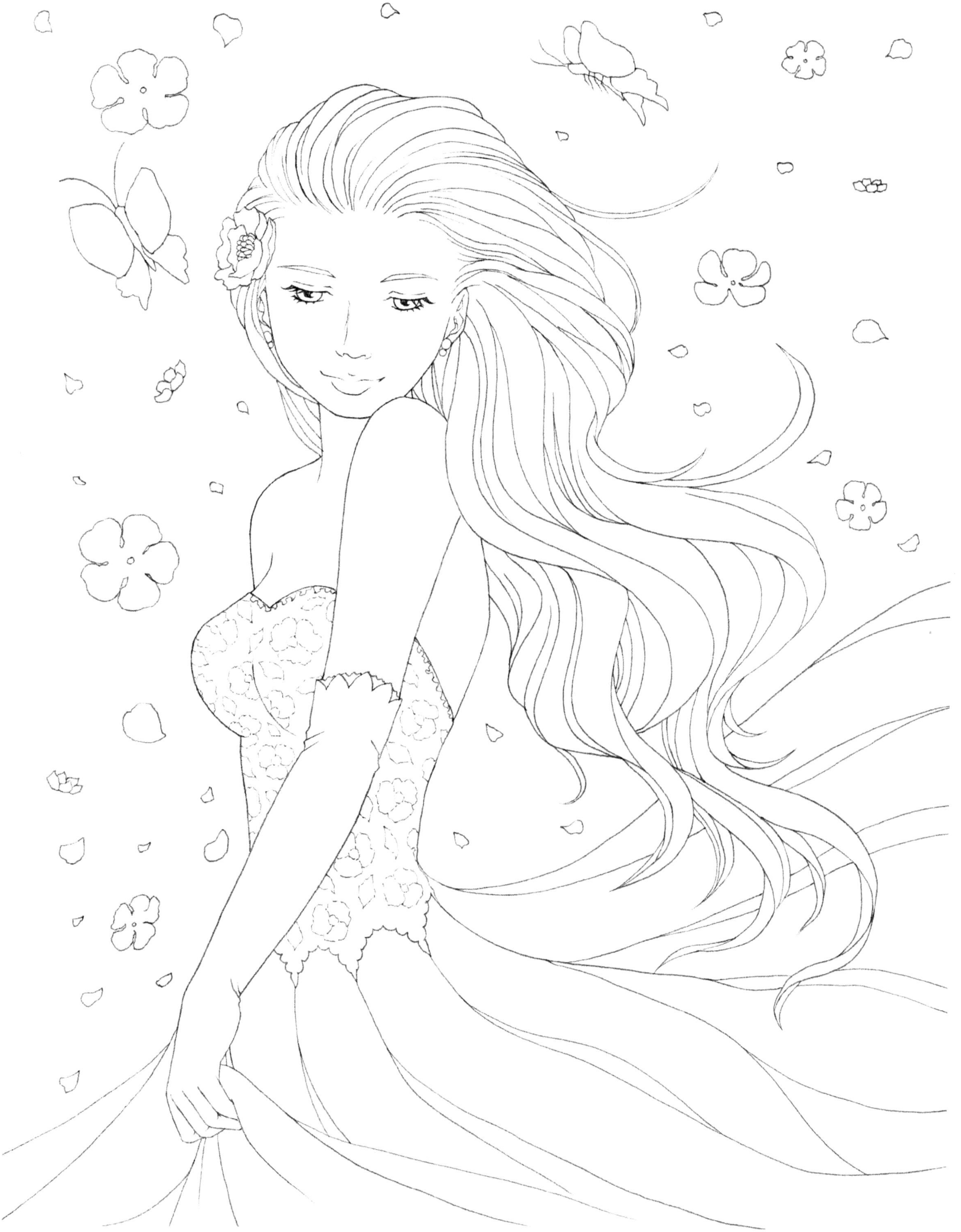

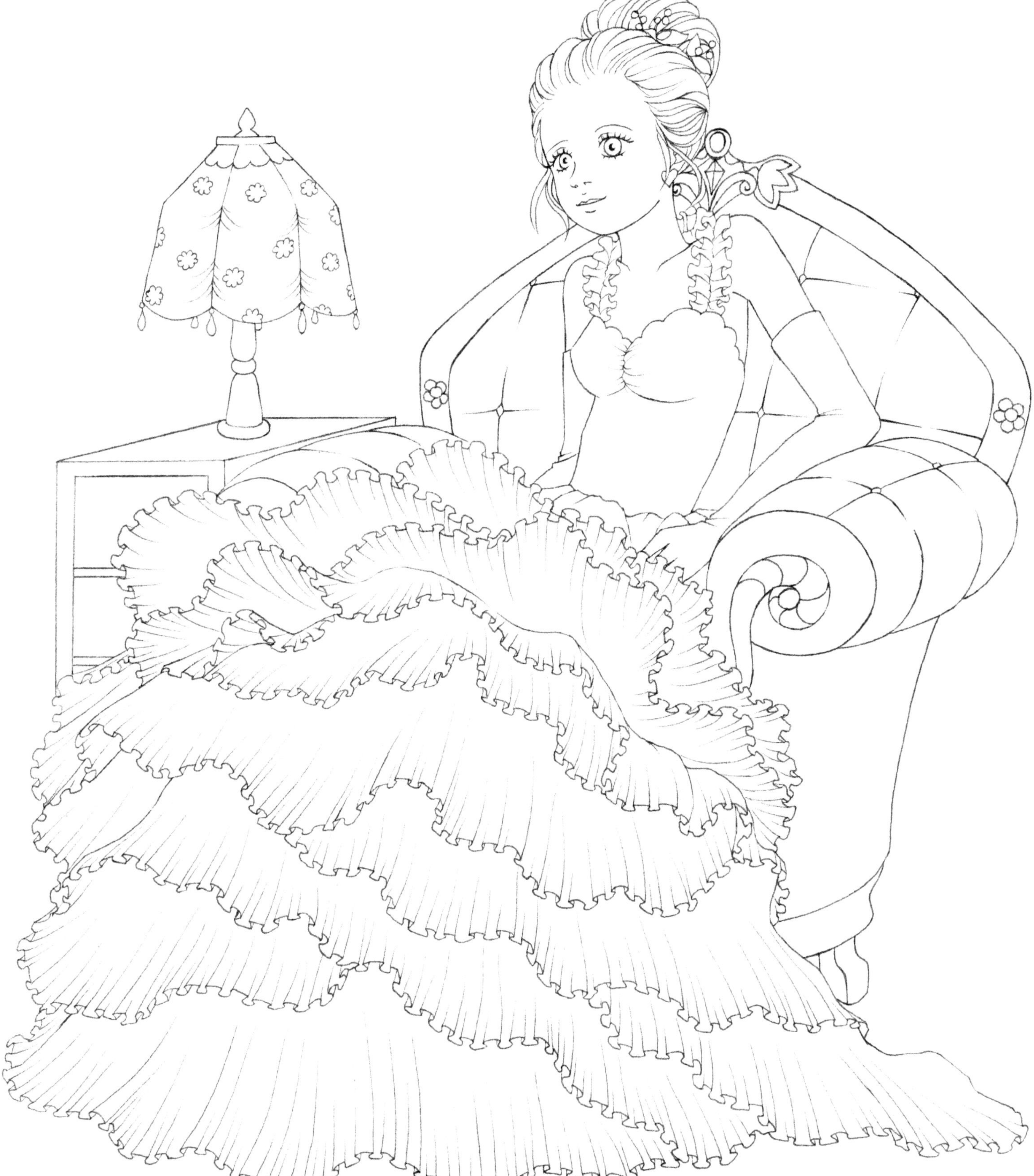

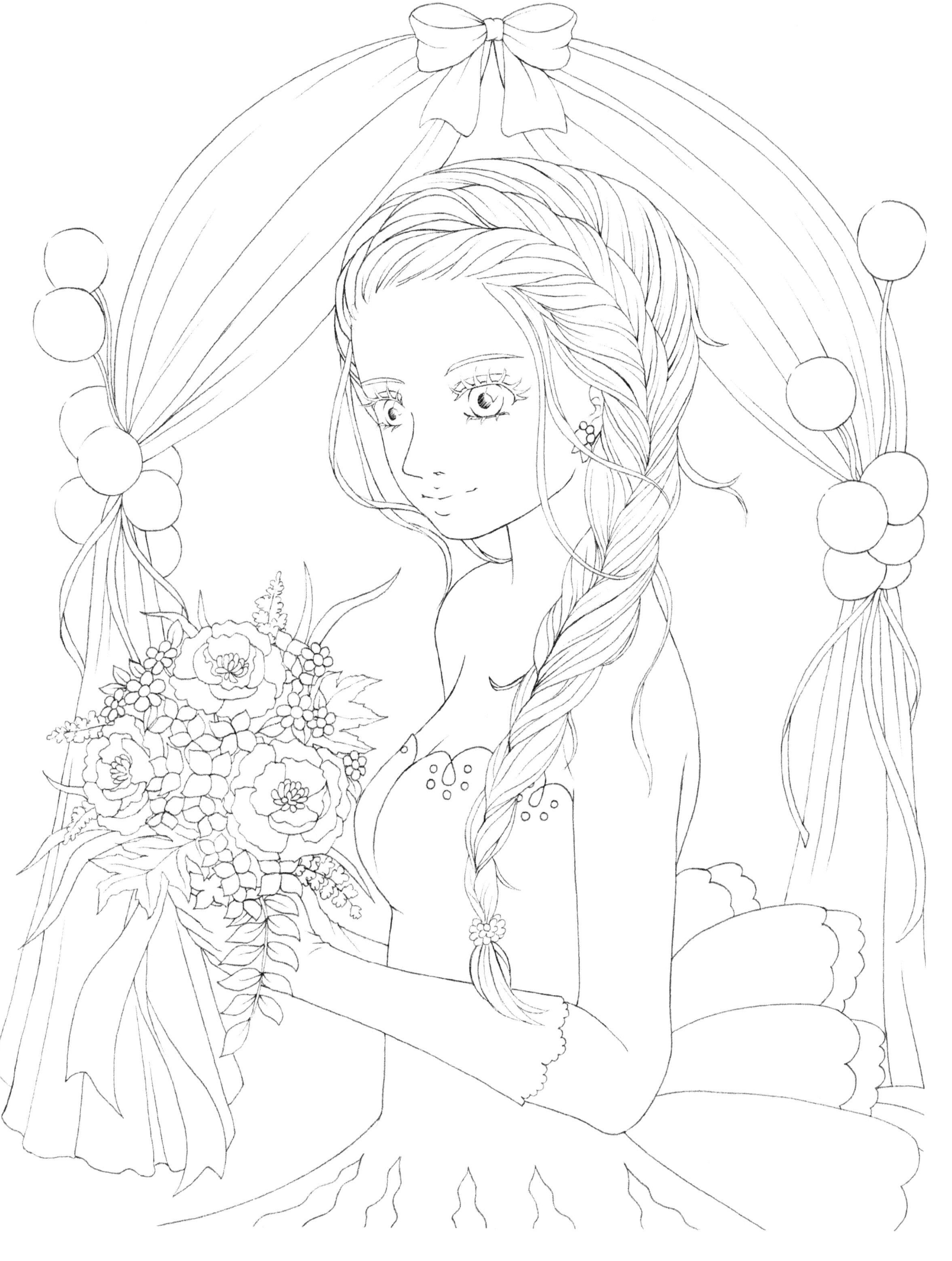

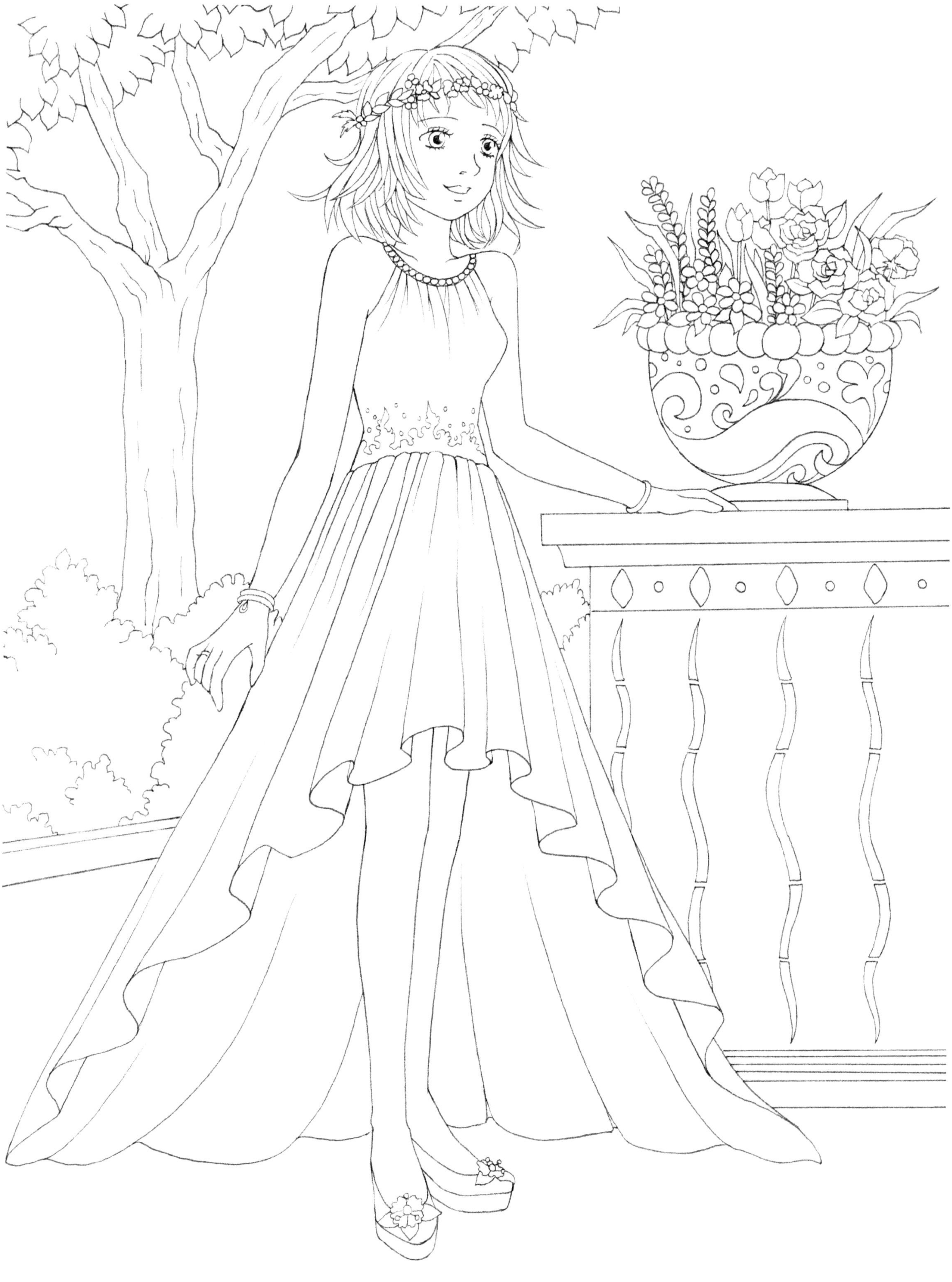

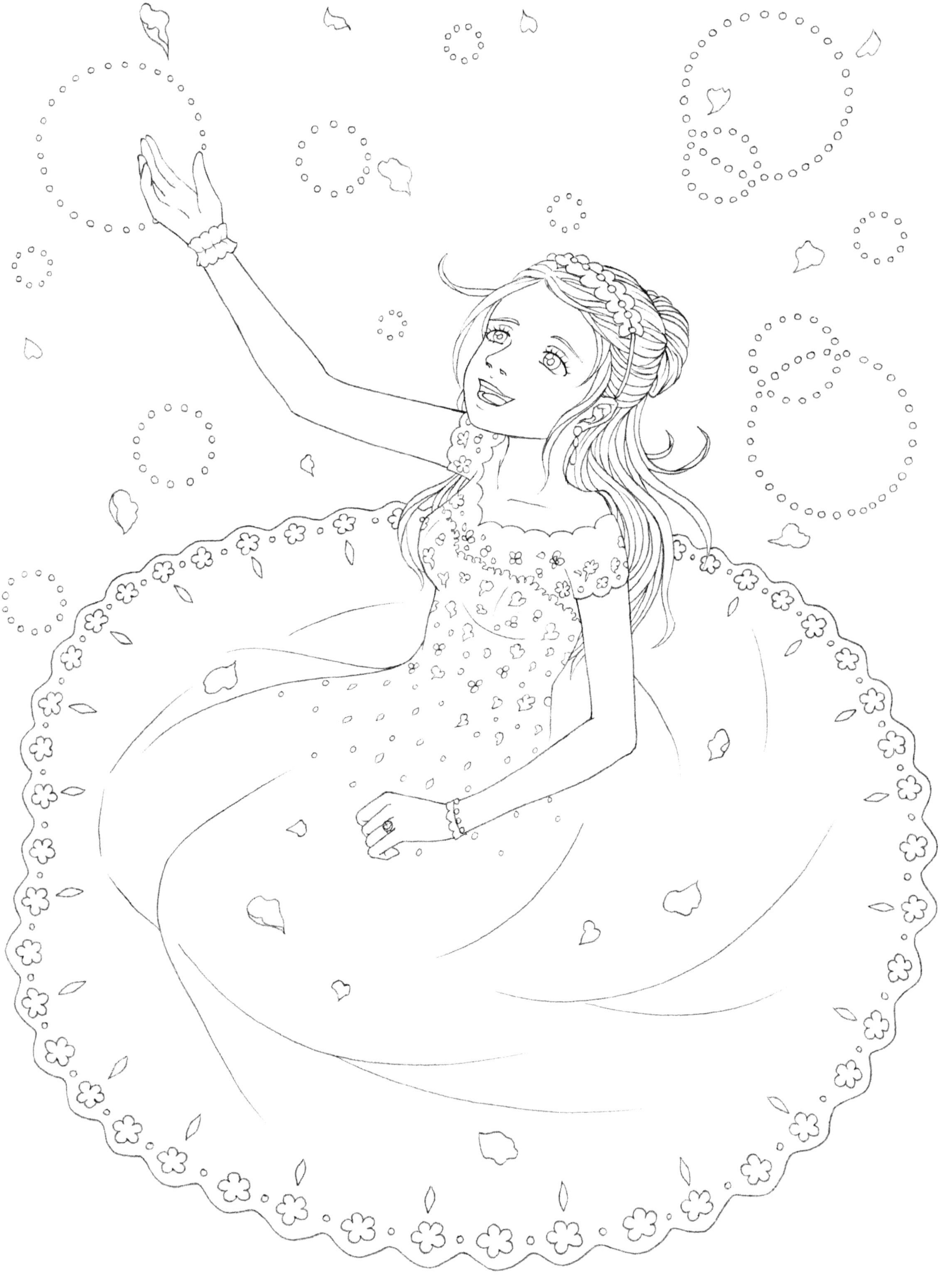

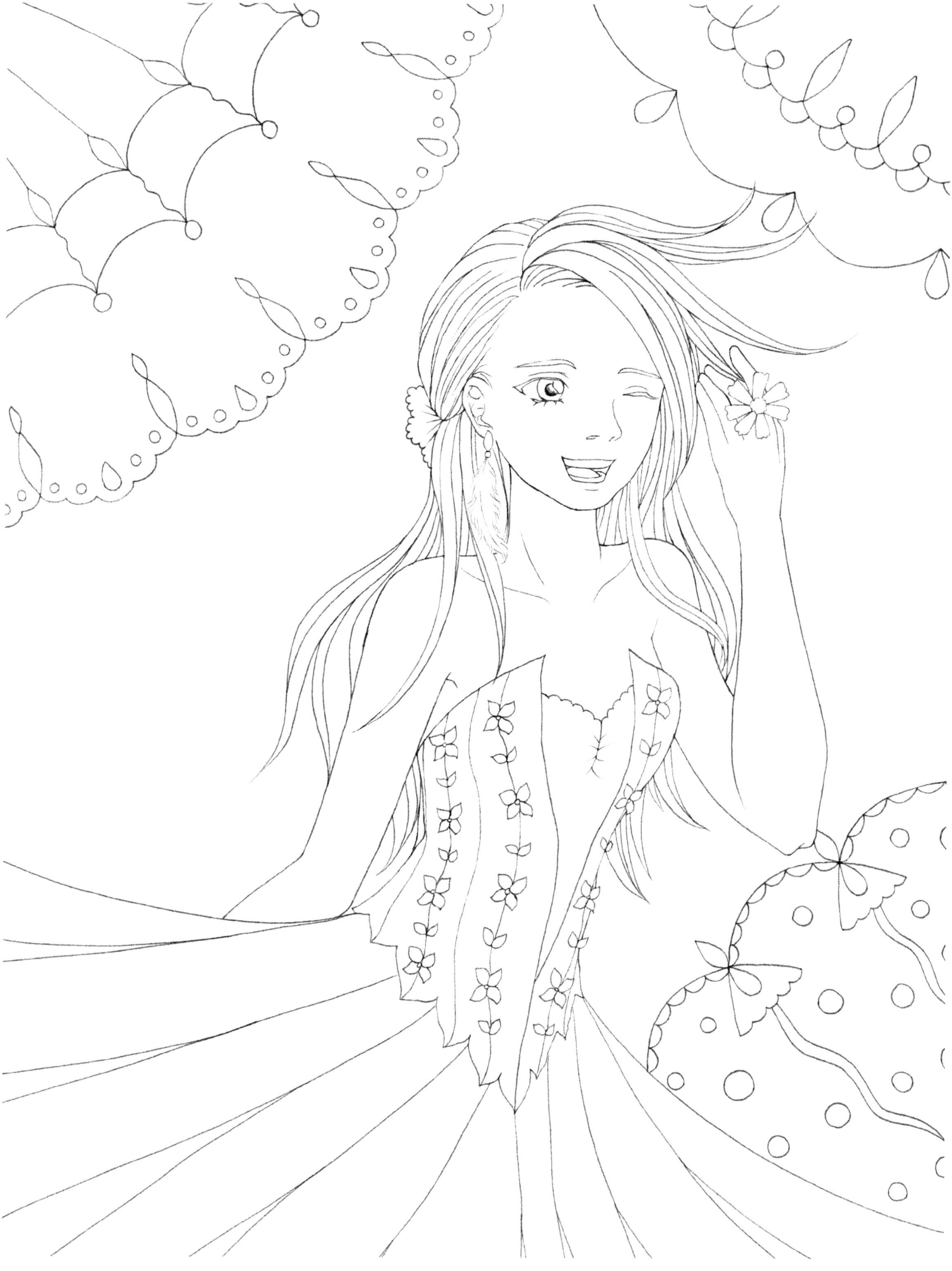

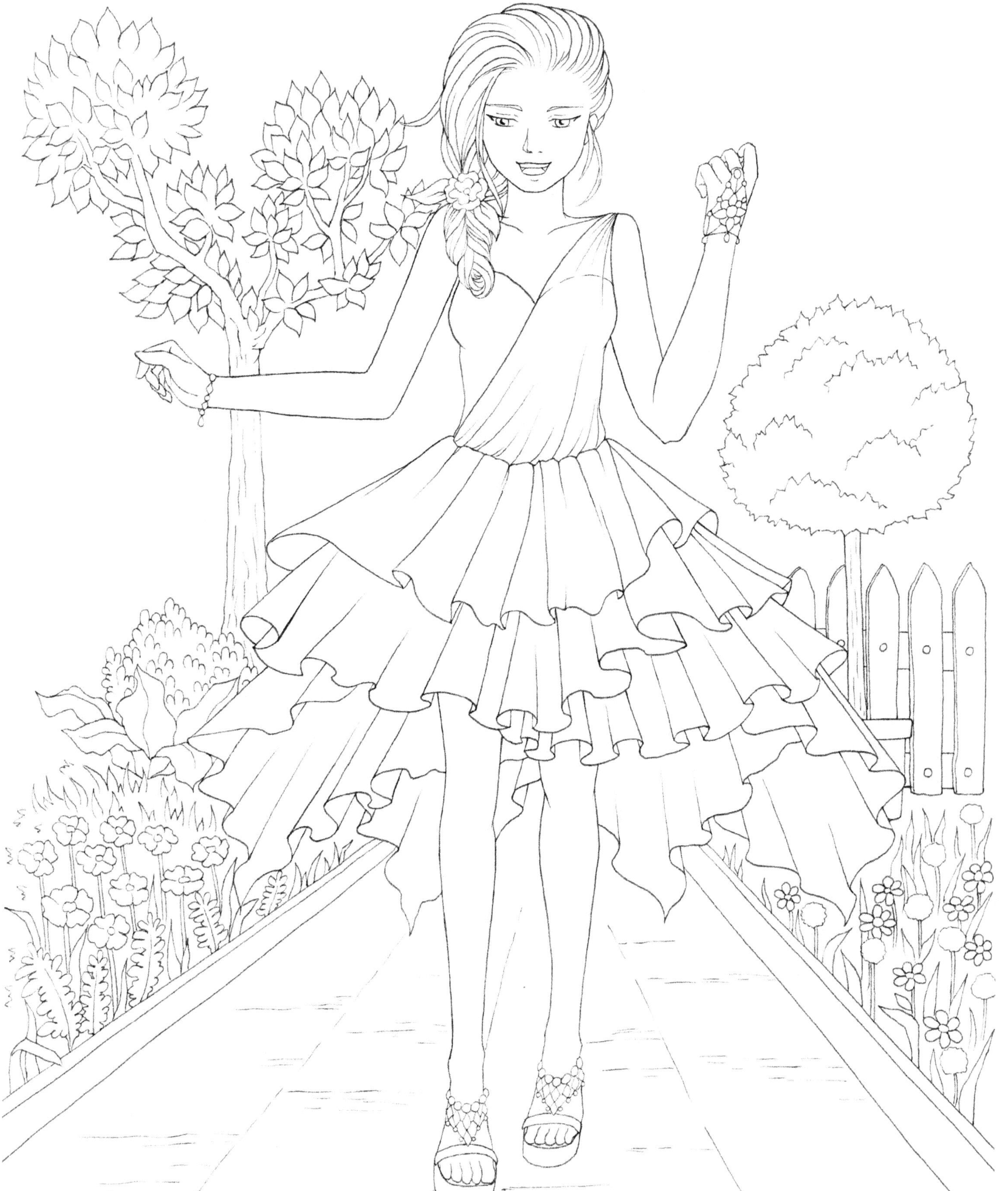

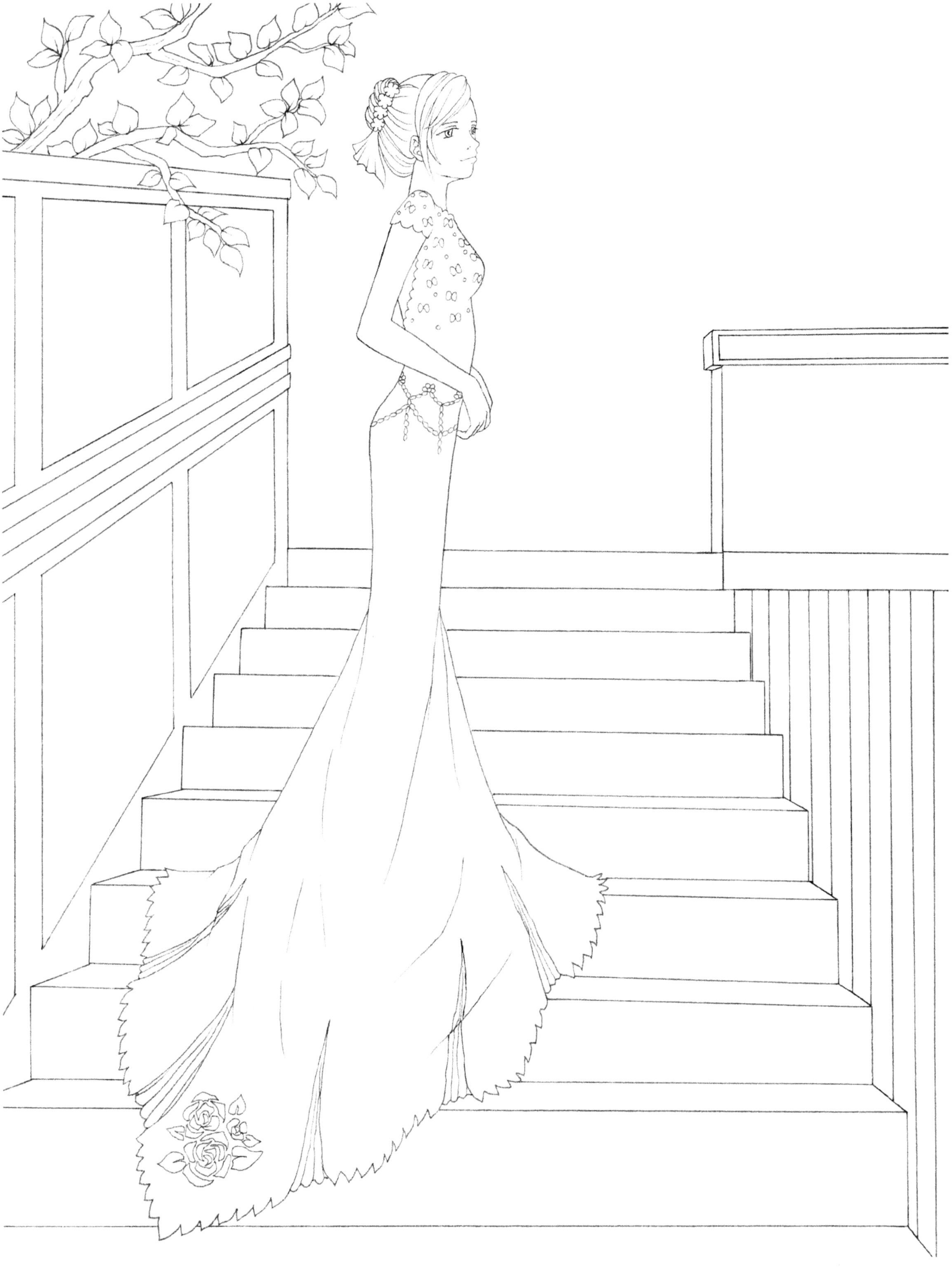

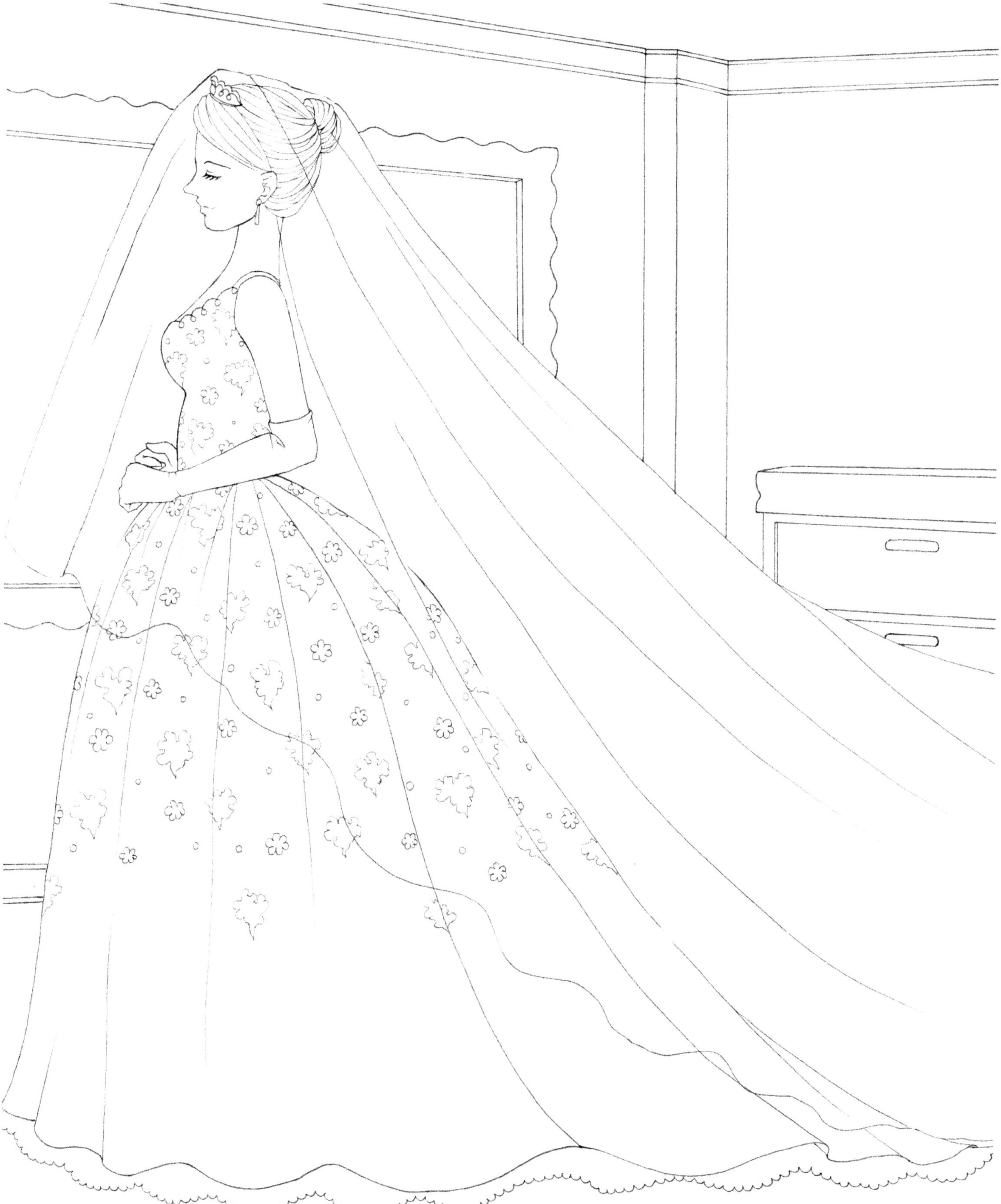

www.ingramcontent.com/pod-product-compliance
Lightning Source LLC
Chambersburg PA
CBHW080605190526
45169CB00007B/2883
* 9 7 8 1 5 3 4 8 9 2 6 8 2 *